THE ALL NIGHT YEMENITE CAFE

Poems by Diane Frank

DARK RIVER PRESS

Davenport, Iowa

ACKNOWLEDGEMENTS

Grateful acknowledgement is made to the following magazines and anthologies in which some of these poems were previously published or accepted for publication: *The Contemporary Review, Yellow Silk, Cimarron Review, Kumquat Meringue, The MacGuffin, Museweek, The Urbanite, Writer's Studio, The Fairfield Journal of Arts and Ideas, Collecting Moon Coins Volume I, Collecting Moon Coins Volume II, Resculpting the Face of God, The Wind Was Late For Breakfast, Prize Poems of the National Federation of State Poetry Societies 1993.*

I want to express my deep appreciation to Kit Redeker for her commitment to publish these poems.

Illustrations - Viktor Tichy
Photograph - Anders Hansen
Typesetting - HIJK, Inc.
Book Design - Kit Redeker
Proofreading - Penny Minkler

Library of Congress Catalog Card Number 93-079492
ISBN 1-884226-01-9

Printed in the United States.

DARK RIVER PRESS
P.O. Box 4547
Davenport, Iowa 52808.

CONTENTS

WILD ORCHIDS

VIDEO ANGEL

THE ALL NIGHT YEMENITE CAFE

WILD ORCHIDS

Inseminating the Cows

With a wild and tender look in his eye
he told me that he is the one
who inseminates the cows.
At the only dairy in Iowa
where the cows have names like
Starfire Sari, Utopia, Aranyani,
and Eternal St. Faye,
they use semen from a bull with
87 daughters,
all good milk producers, he said.
You have to do it at the precise moment
when they are ready,
about 12 hours after they go into heat.
How do you know, I asked him.
He smiled. He said,
most of them go into heat together.
They play in rings
and even mount each other.
Utopia usually gets them started.
He said their personality totally changes.
Sita, for example,
normally a shy girl,
got so excited when she was in heat last year
that she repeatedly mounted the bull.
He winked at me. He said,
I loved to watch them playing
but never saw them complete.
The bull had several children,
but they must have mated in the evening
or in a secret place.
Maybe he was a woman, I said,
in a previous life, and still shy.
But they sold the bull last autumn,
and now, he proudly told me,
they use semen from the best prize bull
in the country.
Ten dollars a straw.
Frozen to 323 degrees below zero
in liquid nitrogen
and ready to go.

1

After the cows go into heat,
you check the mucus.
When they're ready, it's long and stringy
and falls completely down to the ground.
First you put a glove on
all the way up to the shoulder,
and put your hand up her anus
to feel the uterus.
It feels a certain way when they're ready,
firm and toned,
and you know.
Then you take a straw in your other hand,
and gently put it up her vagina.
You have to find the cervix.
It's wet, hard, and cartilaginous
like a woman's. A human cervix
feels something like the bottom of your nose.
Well, a cow's is something like that, he said.
You have to find the opening,
which is very small
and sometimes difficult.
Then you insert the straw
in exactly the right place,
deposit the semen,
and you massage her uterus
for a while with your other hand
so it will take.
Then you know the act is complete
and you leave the cows dreaming
of strong bulls and loving afterplay.
As he tells me, his farmer's hands
are around me
and he massages my left foot
in slow circles
as we lie on my Japanese bed.
I wonder how many men
could describe a human woman's body
with such tenderness and accuracy.
I wonder if he would make
as good a father for human babies.
And he is wondering
about the shapes of everything
inside my white Victoria's Secret nightgown.

The Omen

Four weeks before the snow came,
a calf was born.
You called me,
said her time was ready,
and ran with me out of the barn
to the edge of a field
I had never seen before.

Her feet were sticking out
when we arrived,
then the small tongue.
In one huge contraction
Ila's tail stood straight up.
Then she lay down on the yellow alfalfa grass
below a late October sun
and pushed her calf out.

The calf lay on the ground
not moving
her small eyes open
covered in membrane,
not yet completely in this world.
Then Ila licked her calf all over
with her huge mother's tongue,
pushing her over and over
with her nose
to awaken every cell of her new body.

Slowly, the small one pushed
through membrane after membrane
became more and more alive
pushed her little head up
moved her legs
fell over
pushed up
tried to stand
stood up
and looked around
with completely trusting eyes.

We saw the life go in her
breath by breath.
You called her Namrita,
Sanskrit for "Good Omen."

I watched you milk her mother,
the muscles of your back rippling
like the hills and valleys of late October.
You said Namrita could see
but didn't know what anything was.
I watched you fill a bottle
with her mother's first milk
and feed her.

And when you let me hold the bottle,
much too big for a human baby,
I felt something explode
deep inside my body.

We slept in the barn that night
with a hundred yellow roses in a bucket.
I couldn't leave the calf alone.
It was such a big change for her
coming into this world.

Now your strong hands make me remember
everything I love about this body,
the shepherd on the hills above Jerusalem,
the Goddess in the Egyptian temple.
In the deepest part of my sleep,
I come crashing through
the border of a new country.
A wall of snow
falls at my feet.

Your hands are full of light.
You take your place in the inner circle
of my closest friends —
half in this world
half at the door
of something more.

A Poem about Insects

After the barn dance in Iowa City
(the first of many times
we didn't get along),
there were cockroaches in my bedroom
when I got home —
huge black waterbugs
of the hearty Midwest variety
hiding in the corners of my bedroom,
lounging in the mahogany inlaid box with my jewelry,
sliding down the strings of my guitar,
and crawling between my sheets
instead of you.

From that point on
whenever we had a fight or you disappointed me,
there was a cockroach in my room
or a nightmare variety spider,
large and black.
Sometimes I couldn't sleep in my room for days.

When you were warm and loving,
on nights when you took me to the barn
to feed the calves,
danced with me,
or walked with me
through fields of shoulder-high Iowa weeds,
holding me close to you,
my room was always clear.

"Just tell him 'you bug me,'
when he acts like that,"
a wiser friend advised.
It will get this out of your subconscious
and then maybe the insects will disappear.

I watched you open and close
for nine months
like a tiger lily who couldn't decide
if he wanted to be orange.
I planted flowers around my heart

while you decided if you loved me.
I gave you twenty chances.

The night I became convinced
that things were over between us,
there was a total eclipse of the moon.
In the synergy of the event,
I got locked out of my apartment
and decided to stay at the house of a friend.
Of course, the small room she gave me to sleep in
was infested.
I counted fifty of those little critters,
an exotic tropical variety
with bright orange stripes on their backs and wings,
and even though we hadn't talked about a decision,
I knew that we were through.

As I slept in a quiet space without dreams,
I felt the shadow of the moon across my heart.

Two nights later
I dreamed I was a Cherokee princess
and traveled to the Lower World
in a painted canoe.
When I climbed onto the shore,
I was greeted by every healer I knew,
an entire tribe of medicine men,
and a snow leopard.
As I walked deeper into the forest,
I found you by the small fire
that you keep alone.
You asked me to hold you.
You wanted me to love you,
which surprised me.
You even held my hand
when you walked me back to my canoe.

But you had to let me go
because we live up here
where people aren't as honest about what they need,
where fires are too small,
where rooms are infested with insects.

The Fleas

I can't get rid of them.
We place the RAID foggers
in each room of the house,
haunted by stone soap
and poison gas in concentration camps.
I yell, "Go!"
and in less than five seconds
we set them off
and run out of the house laughing.
Eight hours later
I open the windows,
set the fans spinning,
dream that my ankles have stopped itching.
But in the morning, eight stragglers
still leaping across the bedroom floor
on trampolines, in Reeboks.

Take 2:

I split them with my fingernails,
attach their evasive tiny black bodies
to masking tape,
trap them between two fingers
and flush them down the toilet.
Tiny dark nightmares
that sling-shot into the souffle,
distorting the topology of earlobes,
a mosquito bite over the heart,
gardenias in the champagne glass
along with two mating silverfish,
persistent as the cockroaches
in my mother's fuzzy slipper
the time she came to visit me.
I just can't escape.

Take 3:

The visiting hockey team is ahead.
Fleas: 832.
Me: Nothing.

They are like a street gang
high on cocaine,
stealing ten-year-old cars.
I try to get away,
walking up and down the long palm hills
of Dolores Street
in the late morning.

All the neighborhood dogs
are rolling on my Persian carpet,
leaving microscopic guests
for me to deal with after midnight.
The SWAT team is crawling over the peonies,
hopping from flower to flower.
9-1-1 doesn't help.
At 2:00 in the morning,
they're breaking into my window.

Take 4:

Note to my subconscious:

In the garden of a poet
on Albion Street,
I am far away from the symphony
of late night invaders.
We inhale roses:
Intrigue, Purple Passion,
Happy, Olympiad, White Lightning,
Madame Alfred Perrier,
Love Me —
their scented secrets soft as melons
creamy, pink and sprawling.

I run my fingers
over the richly inflated arms of succulents,
the green oval contours of jade plants,
tracing the geometry of cactus
with my dream infected eyes.

Your cottage full of book clutter,
letterpress art,
and a jazz piano with scars of the heart

that reflects your hands
and your face
as your back softly arches
over the winding violet shades
of your music.

On the music stand,
the calligraphy
of a Vietnamese Buddhist monk
in the late morning sunlight:
"Mindfulness must be engaged."

I engage mindfulness
like the spray paint
in a back alley in the Mission:
"Love me, Lucinda."
"Call me, Nina."
And as I follow
the lacework path of sunlight and shadow
as it weaves around the wooden stairways
and back porches of the Mission,
I let my heart fill itself
with the street music
of the early afternoon,
a soft urban melody,
lifting me back to a place
where it doesn't take my adrenalin
over an hour to shut down,
a refuge without heartache
or fleas.

Dancing by myself
within the soft geometry
of what I have learned to trust,
I arabesque,
leap up
and stay in the air.

Message to the fleas:
You can leave now.

The Lame Man Leaning on the Mailbox

Old Ed asked his family
to send his ashes back to Nebraska —
the farmland that he loved.
I'd been thinking about showing him
photographs of the Midwest
where I live now,
the prairie house that I own,
my favorite heifer
named after the Goddess of the Moon,
long rows of Mama cows being milked
with a spiritual light
almost too bright to look at
washing over them from the barn door.
I kept thinking I'd go and visit
in two or three days,
but I was too late.

All of us in the apartment building on Church and 28th
remember Ed leaning on the mailbox —
belly leaning out over his suspenders
the smiling man
the lame man in front of the toy store window.
When I came back to San Francisco that summer,
one of my neighbors told me
that Ed had been on oxygen for months.
It kept getting harder and harder for him to breathe
until his last breath was gone.

Big Ed used to flirt with all the women
in the neighborhood.
Brown skinned Latina teenagers
with flowing black hair and designer jeans,
winos, widows
old women trekking down the 28th Street hill
to buy groceries every afternoon
at the corner store owned by Palestinians.
I watched their faces light up
under the netting of old hats
left over from nightclubs in the '40s.

When my mother came to visit me in San Francisco,
Ed fell in love with her instantly.
He even had the cockroaches exterminated to impress her.
She couldn't walk down the hallway of our building
without basking in the moonlight
of his toothy smile —
the big smile
that always came to his face
when I mentioned her name.

Crusty old man.
He used to be a dancer.
One afternoon he had to show me.
Jitterbug
waltz
tango
dancing sideways down the hall
next to the carved bannister.
For a few moments
my 98 pounds were captive
to that huge suspendered body.

When his health started to fail
everyone in our building
hid it from the management.
Even the old nurse with cancer
stopped complaining.
Michael fixed anything
that went wrong in the apartments.
During the earthquake he turned off the water,
gas, and electricity for the whole building.
He told me he went to every apartment
one by one
to make sure everyone was all right
while his books slid off the shelves
and collected in a heap on the floor
large enough for a bonfire,
while his plates and silverware
rattled out of the cabinets
and collided with one another
on the way to the floor,
while Robin's hot water heater
emptied itself

and trickled down
from apartment to apartment
until it flooded the bottom floor.

Then he took Ed to the fire station
with his oxygen tank
so he would be able to breathe
in an emergency.
We didn't want to risk losing him
while all of the other fires were burning.

The day I left California
only eight months before
it was snowing all the way down the coast.
It was the first time I'd seen snow
for ten years,
and as I was crossing the desert
I had a quiet feeling
that I was escaping something terrible.
Then I forgot.
I would have been in the BART station
while my books were crashing
into my glass animals
and my photographs fell down.

Summer in San Francisco.
My neighbors told me
they didn't want Ed taken to a county home
where they'd drug him until he lost
his will to live.
We all wanted him here
with us
to tell his corny jokes
and complain about our habits
in the torn carpet halls
that smelled like my grandfather's
first apartment in this country.
We lied and told the social workers
that everything was all right.

Now Old Ed is flying.
His body is full of light.
Smoke and ashes
float upwards
white as the snow
in the land where he was born.
Birds of moonlight
surround him now
above the alfalfa fields
where the landscape changes color.

Geometry of a Neon City

"We go where we need to go, and then try
to figure out what we're doing there."
— Jeff Greenwald
Shopping for Buddhas

I live on the street with the palm trees
in the Mission District,
18 blocks south of the oldest Spanish church in the city,
two miles west of the Twin Peaks tower
where the local wino philosophers
have predicted the spaceships will come
and carry us away
if we forget to recycle our garbage.

Welcome to Neon City.
I am a tourist in the city where I used to live
away from the land of the
not so sacred cows.

Most of my neighbors
come from Central America,
with a spiral melody of Chinese,
Vietnamese and Pilipino.
When you go to the market,
it's tortillas, tomatoes,
ayote, kabocha, camote —
bargaining weaving through boom boxes
blasting in Spanish.

Every part of me
that was cramped beneath the stubblefields
of the long Midwestern winters
is dancing,
hiking at Point Reyes through fields of lupines,
spinning counterclockwise at Ashkenaz,
seeing all the friends I gathered
for the past ten years,
having a picnic at Stern Grove
while the fog is floating away
from the eucalyptus trees.

14

Welcome to the geography of calla lilies,
the geometry of Dolores Street.
Welcome to mango paletas
at Latin Freeze after work.
Welcome to acrobats
dressed in the colors of Chinese kites
over a valley of street music.

I stay up so late
it makes my telephone number disappear.
Last week when my dance partner
tried to call,
he got an old Japanese woman
above a vegetable market.
She could barely speak English
but she laughed and laughed.
Then she told him she wanted
to be reincarnated as a cat.

At night, the neon geometry
reminds me of a distant planet —
wild and friendly shapes and colors,
blue cafes,
red sushi bars,
chartreuse asteroid chips,
pink flamingos
on neon planetoid rings.

Welcome to Neon City —
the deep river
with the colorful fish
of my dreams,
the old woman knitting sweaters
for everyone she can get her hands on,
the local bag lady
sleeping on the park bench
in front of the toy store.

My dance partner gives me an orange
and asks me to eat it like a poet.
The music dances through him,
and he's always asking for more.
He wants me to tell him a story
with every sacred atom in my body.

I'm trying to find a way
to come up with two bodies
so I can do everything,
and you know it's more than dancing.

Welcome to Neon City —
palm trees
outside my window
on the balmiest street in town,
the wind threading the fog
around the coconuts,
through the branches,
dancing all night
in a symphony of forgiveness.

How to Jumpstart a Dream

1.
Rainbow ribbons are rippling
in a wind
formed by a vortex of dreams.

Look for something hanging
by a window,
a Japanese fern,
banners with messages
or lead crystals.

Blow into them.
Create movement
before you dissolve into the vision
on the other side.

2.
Look for the reflection of tiny stars
in an amethyst crystal,
and watch the delicate
points of light
move
as you step backwards.

Line up geodes
at the foot of your bed.

Find the color missing
from the rainbow
reflected by a hidden light,
and follow it
until the asteroid particles
blur.

3.
Follow the images in your photographs
into the light of a foreign country.
Cross over a suspended bridge
to the Kali Gandaki River gorge
and walk on the other side
of the river.

Follow a row of prayer flags
into the air.

Pose asymmetrically
on top of a mountain in Tibet
and follow the spindrift
up to the moon.

4.
Rub oils scented with jasmine
or coconut
into your skin.
Follow the edges
of your elbows and knees,
the scent of a balmy wind
blowing up from the south.

Angels with glass wings will guide you.
Ask them questions,
even if you can't see them.

Use your pinky
to trace a spiral on your belly.
Listen for melodies
in the musical curve in the small
of your back.
Follow the half moons
on both sides of your heart
into the sky.

5.
Light a beeswax candle
inside the tin lantern
that reflects snowflakes all over the sky
of the silent place where you sleep.

Put cinnamon, cardamom, ginger
into your midnight tea.
Drink it slowly
and follow the winding journey
of the water
as it melts into your body.

Let your edges expand
into snowflakes
as you melt into sleep.

6.
Put your left hand softly
over the spinning wheel of your heart
and fall asleep
loving all the unfinished places
of your journey into the unknown.

When you wake up
another piece of what
you have been searching for
will fly into your throat
softly, like a bird
made of starlight.
Sing back to her
before you turn the corner
behind the mirror.

Gifts

A small opening
between us
in the shadows we reflect
on the wall —
a heart, a bone.

We play tag in the water,
and I keep
letting him catch me.

I show him photographs —
dark hair falling
past my shoulders,
slender legs
wrapping around a cello,
and he remembers.

He points
to where I was looking
when the music stopped
and says, "Up here."

Pale blue jeans
softly sculptured
on the floor.

I trace the bones
connected
like wings
behind his shoulders
with my smallest finger.

Now I feel the light
on my lips.

Wild Orchids

I want to think of the men I love
like stones I find at the beach —
the ones at Ano Nuevo
at the private beach
beyond the "No Trespassing" sign.
That's where you find the rocks
with the seashell fossils
in a secret place.

I want to be able to pick them up
and put them down
without sorrow,
like a wild orchid
I leave where it is growing.

That would be the way
to let go
like a starfish or a moonshell,
curved, spotted like a leopard,
floating on a rivulet through the sand
all the way out to the ocean —
letting go
the way the Buddhist monks
I met high up in the mountains in Nepal
taught me.

The echo of your face still orbits around me
like a familiar planet.
I can't forget
the blue grey of your eyes
full of fear and longing,
your arms
reaching for me
out of the center of an Egyptian prayer,
your strong legs
with muscles curved like shells,
and the "No Trespassing" sign.

In the late hours of the evening
I surround myself with words.
They fill up with salt water and sing,
and they make me strong.
I learn so much from my failures
that I have to bless them.
Sometimes I think we are all
intricate patterns of shell inside rock,
glowing with the memory of ancient lives.

I want to be waist high
in calla lilies,
up to my elbows
in birds of paradise
orange as the California sun
on a path leading out to the ocean
just before sunrise.
I want to sing
until I forget
the meaning of sorrow.

VIDEO ANGEL

The Promise

I turn on the light
and leave the door open
full of roses,
but it doesn't seem to be enough —
at least not right now.

I've been dancing with an invisible partner.
My dreams say I will meet him one day.
In the pyramids,
we were dressed in peacock feathers,
a band of gold around his head
and mine.
When I was sleeping,
I felt him hold my heart,
but I couldn't see his face.

Tonight
I am the question in your pocket,
silent music floating around your heart,
denied entry.
In a dream
the scent of gardenias
as intoxicating as your body,
yellow as a rose,
soft as the light
that comes from your hands.

In a new season
roses break through the dry and brittle earth,
pink and yellow
like an ancient promise.
One day they will all be pink.
I've been told
the one from the pyramids
will come to me
with a long-stemmed yellow rose,
and I will see his face.

Video Angel

On Mt. Shasta
I met somebody I felt I had known
for five thousand years.
"You've always felt like you're from another planet?"
he asked me. "You are," he said, "and I come
from the same place.
Even my wife doesn't understand."

I've been fighting alienation
for as long as I can remember.
"I came to tell you so you wouldn't be so lonely,
so you could at least partially understand."
But after each love letter explodes,
I don't understand.

During the convergence
there was a video angel on TV.
There were skeptics, believers
and people who thought she was just
some cheap electronic trick.
But if you sang or chanted to her,
she got brighter. She even laughed sometimes,
and you felt it in your heart.
She was the same kind of angel you see in meditation,
the kind that comes to lift your burden
or heal you
when the weight of this planet becomes too great.

Like a video trick
she slipped down the antenna,
stepping up the current to 30,000 volts,
and softening it at the same time —
translating chrominance and luminance
to angel form
so everyone could see her.

After the weekend
my friend went back to his wife.
I went back to my students,
avoided outer space,

ran away from its prickly afterimages.
We planted cactus in our sleep
and they sprouted in our dreams.
Later arms and legs appeared,
but we didn't dare
to touch this alien creature.

Sometimes I remember the planet that we came from.
In the small hours of the night,
I see the forms and faces,
and it fills me with a private joy.
Then, I feel like a video angel —
a celestial electron beam signal
spreading her wings in public.

Lunar Eclipse

I couldn't tell if he was hiding light
in shadows
or something dark
trying to be an angel.

We were wandering in a garden of poison flowers
opium poppies and belladonna
a red shadow floating
a soft light the color of wheat
rippling inside my body.

Our whispered words
expressed a kindred madness.
The music was totally improvised
in a language I don't understand
but can feel with my body
like a blind woman
in a garden of sculpture.

She doesn't even know what day it is
only the language of touching flowers
pulsing yellow through the fingertips
or the music of lips touching
thighs filled with foreign melodies.

He said I seduced him with my thoughts,
but he seduced me with his hands
while my voice was breaking.

We sat in silence,
then he put a blanket over my shoulders.
It made me shiver.

Field mice were skittering
inside walls of canvas.
The man had dissolved
into a night of grasshoppers
into the hills outside my window.

His moods outnumbered me —
shadows lost from the language of wolves
just below the skin
too far away.

Under the Crust of the Huckleberry Pie

He wanted to seduce her,
but she felt like she was being compared
to something invisible —
the geometry of a dream,
wisteria on the wooden gate,
the half-life of plutonium.

It wasn't that he didn't love her.
He noticed the definition of her legs
under the black lace,
strong from years of dancing,
strong from walking over mountains.
They danced after midnight,
hips swaying rhythmically to Cajun music,
his thumb in the back pocket
of her velvet jeans
and another woman's smile.

He came close to her
like a zebra
before he runs back into the forest,
a barn before it burns,
with the synchronicity of a spider
under the kerosine lamp on the back porch,
tulips beside the terra cotta swan.

He said he wanted more
but held back,
the glass sinews of his shoulders
a pattern of vectors
in a garden of oxalis,
silver canoes crossing a lake
through peacock feathers
in a thunderstorm.

She covered his wounds with honeysuckle,
but he wanted something invisible,
light reflecting off the piano
into different shades of silence.

She sang to him
as they walked through a stand of aspens,
the fine strands of his hair
gold in the sunlight.

She said, "I want to cover your mouth
with kisses
like red leaves,
red leaves falling from a half open window
with music from a balalaika,"
but his shoulders were still made of glass.

Photograph from Okinawa

In the photograph
she is coming down the stairs
from the bath house where she lives.
You are the 19-year-old Marine
from North Carolina
whose words flow into her ears
like an exotic song
from the other side of a mystery.

You are tall, handsome
and the wide muscles of your arms
push into the seams of your shirt
before you scatter your uniform
on her tatami floor.

She is lost in the cornflower blue
of your eyes as you rock
her narrow bed
and fill the halls of the bath house
with cat sounds.

And in the geisha curves
of her perfect island body
you are trying to forget the daylight
of the military base
where you don't have a voice.

When you ask her to smile
for the photograph
you don't notice the way
her eyes are glazing over the pain
she feels every time she remembers
the soldier who went to Vietnam
and exploded one afternoon
in the middle of the jungle
in a cloud of orange fire.

And you are unaware
that moments before you leave this island
for the last time

she will try to fold herself
in your suitcase.

A week later
two of your friends will tell you
that they found her at midnight
running naked down the street.

When they bring her back
to the bath house
she will dream she is eight years old
trying to dig a tunnel to North Carolina
with a silver spoon.

She has no idea
that twenty years later
after your round-eye wife
breaks all of your dishes
and walks out of your house
for the last time,
after your next girlfriend
is dragged out of her apartment in Manhattan,
tied up, and thrown into a suitcase,
after five pilgrimage journeys
to holy places in the Himalayas
at altitudes beyond where
the people you've left behind can breathe,
and the other woman you have finally come to love
walks out of your house for the last time
and won't even answer your phone calls,
you will find her photograph.

She doesn't know
that you worship her now
inside a golden frame
beside your paintings of bodhisattvas
and holy stones from the Ganges River.

She has no idea
how much you loved her,
and you didn't either
at the time.

Night Conversations

Rabbits at night
silhouetted against the prairie sky,
their soft, white forms
arched like Egyptian heiroglyphs.
You talk to the rabbits.
They answer you in silence.

You say form is everything.
It contains all the passion.
Clay becoming cubist under your hands.
A piano finely tuned
to the contours of your body.

In your small room
with the tatami mat on the floor,
you make a salad.
I don't say anything.
I dream I am floating into you.
I dream I am shaping dough.

You say our relationship
has changed in subtle ways
since the Berlin Wall came down.
Every day we touch it differently.

I feel you
rubbing a secret code
into my body,
brushing the Sumi-e ink tones of wild horses
into my wrists,
planting messages
in the soles of my feet
with your fingertips,
my spine stretching
to flying rings of bone.

Every note of music
sounds like you just discovered it —
its tactile
thoughts forming a body.

What I Told the Squirrels Last Night

The squirrels are absolutely obese tonight —
blubbing around the backyards,
falling off trees,
waltzing on the roof of the shed
like beached whales.
They don't know what to do with the nuts.

I walk outside dressed like a harem dancer.
It's late November,
but bulbs are coming up
out of season,
purple and white
under the streetlamps.

Now I'm spinning like ragweed,
intoxicated by the smell
of red and yellow leaves.

Southern winds come in
carrying every single flower
since the Gulf of Mexico.

I want it sultry all winter
with the Swan Lake music of oboes
in the air all night,
gardenias
under a blue jazz moon.

A mist sets in
over a glow of colored lights
too early for December.
An electric wind blows blue
against the farmhouse across the field.

The clouds are swimming
like fish scales full of light
while the mud breaks into small wedges
below my feet.

Pink halo around the moon
and a midnight heat
like an old lover
who almost promises to stay.
The tiny crystals of ice are
up there.

In Solitude

"It's as if the grass in the fields and what's left
of the cornfields is glowing from within."
— Kathleen Ryan

I.

It's snowing in early March
and the tulips are dying —
a wild evaporation of yellow.

I gather the unopened buds
during the thunder blizzard
and bring them inside.

When they open,
they explode into a yellow
so brilliant you can almost
feel the sun in the petals,
but after a few hours
the stems disintegrate from the shock
of having been frozen.

II.

She wore a red leotard
during the massage,
and when she asked him
if he wanted to put his clothes on,
he lit a candle.

The tea they drank
was full of kuchika twigs,
and in the late afternoon
she had to forgive him
for the wound in her throat.

All night long her dreaming
was in the language of gardenias,
but in the morning
the light through the curtain
was red and shocking.

The fortune cookie said,
"Tall Swedish stranger,
unexpected edges,
and a voluptuous layer of sadness
under lace."

But when she read the shape
of the twigs in his teacup,
she felt like someone else
was in the room —
someone familiar, but invisible.

III.

As I take my photographs
off the gallery walls,
the open spaces begin to speak:

Just let the place be empty.
Let it be soft as moonlight
in the deep freeze
of an extended winter.

Listen to the glass petals
of the snowflakes as they fall
high on a mountain
without wind,
like the mountain river rhythm
of your own heart
as it softly opens
to its own music.

Everything He Paints
Has Seven Meanings

His hat is falling off his head
as he climbs the fire escape
at 5:00 in the morning.
He is the man with the oregano cigarette
and wild black hair,
on his face
a play of light and shadow.

In the background, a woman
reclines on a crocodile,
her red dress a lava flow,
the sky escaping from her hair.
His father says, "Her face is muddy,
dreadfully realistic.
El Greco painted with light."

The geodesic dome is curved
like a gompa in Tibet
or a flying saucer.
Three flying hologram rays
in the shape of intergalactic birds
are flying up to Antares
on lasers the shape of nighthawks.
This is where the people from the Pleiades will come.
This is where the birds will paint
with short feathers.
This is where the seasons intersect.

The self portrait of the painter
is pretentious, self-absorbed
with Tahitian puddles blurring into the Pleiades.
A blue mermaid floats into a conch
at right angles
underwater.
At sunrise
she changes herself
into a woman with Gauguin skin
a watermelon dress
and trays of banana fantasies.

He smuggles paints into the geodesic
and spreads them out in the dark,
painting music.
He watches the sunrise
through candles the shape of windows.

Painting number one: Desert succulent
                               green and snakey
                               inside the folds of sleep.
Painting number two: Laser show.
                               Spaceship transformations.
Painting number three: Gauguin woman
                               with a melon dress.
Painting number four: Madonna and Child
                               in orbit.
Painting number five: Baby elephant seals
                               dancing in slow circles.
Painting number six: Mermaids
                               swimming in pointillist shades
                               of pink and purple water.

At midnight he is still painting
the iridescent
half domes of grapes
on their melon arms.
The mermaids, of course, are pregnant.
But his father closes his umbrella,
whispers "Dreadfully realistic"
to the rain.

Cool Jerk in August

The summer I went away to work
at the interracial camp on Bear Mountain,
I came back dancing the "Cool Jerk" to hot music.
The basketball team in the kitchen taught us how.
When I came back to New Jersey and showed my parents,
my father said the dance was dirty,
but he didn't explain
and I didn't know why.
My mother said, "You're a woman now
and you have to be careful,"
but I was sixteen
and didn't know what I had to be careful of.

When Betty, the camp director,
caught three of us shooting the breeze
with the forward line of the soccer team
on the steps of our tent,
she locked us inside her cabin for three days.
She wanted a confession about what else we were doing,
but that wasn't part of my religion.
She said, "On the steps of your tent
is just like kissing a boy in your bedroom,"
but I didn't understand what was wrong with that.

That night, the boys kept hiding
under the floorboards of our tent,
stinking of Jade East
and hoping we would come back.
Ginny whispered to me
that the center forward from the Bronx
put his hand under her shirt.
I whispered back that when Danny and I slow danced,
he sang sweet harmonies in my ear.
He pretended he was a disk jockey from New York,
and I pretended I believed him.

For two-and-a-half days, I kept telling Betty
that I hadn't done anything wrong,
and I completely believed it.

39

We drove her crazy humming "He's So Fine"
with a glazed look in our eyes,
and swearing under our breath
with a few choice words in Spanish
that the Puerto Rican cook taught us.

Maybe it was Betty's buck teeth
or the way her bony knees kept shaking
when she talked,
but late in the afternoon
of the third day of our confinement,
the walls started swimming
and I forgot what I knew.

I went home that summer with a new knowledge.
I sat by myself for hours in back of the school yard
in a varsity jacket three sizes too big
watching the basketball team.
In the silence before the foul shots,
Betty's voice still echoed
labelling me with the "bad girl" crowd.
I still didn't know exactly what that entailed,
but I wore it on my jacket like a medal.

The Woman You Didn't See
in Your Rear View Mirror

— For Annie, in her voice

You almost saw my reflection
in your rear view mirror
while you were feeding strawberries
dipped in chocolate
to my husband
on the swing set in the park.

My bathroom mirror cracks
when I go searching for my lost girl self —
an image stolen by time,
distorted by the stretching and pulling
of my once ballerina waist
by three strong children.

On my wedding night
I gave him the whole vessel
of my young girl's heart.
My hair was long and blonde,
my legs dancer thin,
and I adored him.
Before the moon rose
over the pines below our balcony,
we tied ourselves together
with the soft pink ribbons
of our wedding vows.

The half moon in my belly grew
while he carved a doll house
for our first daughter.
Our love was the wheat,
the ocean, the sky.
I put the seaweed of my girlhood
into the sinews and muscles
of laughing children.

I gave my blueberry eyes
to the sky in my daughter's face.
The folds in my belly you laugh at

41

held his children
and the hidden face of the moon
before I pushed them
out into the late morning sunlight.
Over long years of loving
I gave my children the silk of my hands.
Later my husband complained
that the walls of my birth canal
weren't elastic enough for love.

You are the one who holds my husband now
tight as the stretch
designer jeans you wear.
He says that loving you
makes him feel
he will never grow old.

I know my skin
isn't tight across my cheekbones
the way it used to be,
and my legs are criss-crossed
by the small violet highways of spider veins.
I know you think I'm here to haunt you
like a hag in a children's story.

But when I appear in your dreams
like a lost key
at three o'clock in the morning,
I'm only holding a mirror
for you to look at your future.
I am the waitress in the starched white dress
pouring a cherry Coke
behind the candy counter
at the variety store.
I am asking for compassion,
for love.
The shadow figures you fear
are only your reflection.

But I come to wish you children,
a faithful husband,
and a round painted mirror
for your love.

The Winding Journey
Back to My Right Shoulder

Once again,
I am in the country of people without hands,
where men are looking for apples
on top of glass hills.
Once again, I am falling
down the lazy curves
of an apple shaped hill.
A crunchy taste that evaporated
while I was dreaming.
The unexplored territory
where red dissolves into the intersection of green
on the unbitten skin.

Suddenly I am aware
of a dull ache in my right shoulder
a buzzing sound in the room
the green of my lamb's wool sweater
the black of my calfskin boots
and the taste of leaves in my mouth.
I am not completely awake
wishing to be held while I sleep
so I can fall in more softly
to the bright open space that surrounds
my dreaming.

At 6:00 in the morning
a thin line of light
pushes in through the crack in the door
at the speed that photons of sunlight
hurl themselves through space
to the green and watery leaves
of a cottonwood tree.
My neurons reach and crack
in the link between events
and emotional states.
The dreams I didn't have:
scalding water
inside brass teapots,
a long night in the singing space
where you didn't try to hold me.

A thin line of pain
is stabbing me in my right shoulder.
There's a tightness in my throat
where the swelling of leaves isn't full.
But you break through the membrane of stems
with the white heat of your hands.
Rivers of energy run up my legs
in laser lines of force
pink ribbons untied
at my ankles.

I ask you to see me
as an entry, a window,
a deeper way of seeing yourself.
But it's only the dream
of a three-year-old in the sandbox
with dirty ribbons in her hair.
Late at night
the gypsies laugh at me
with glass voices.
They say it's not the right time.
I have dreams about someone
who is coming later,
but I still can't feel the silver
music of his words
in my shoulders.

The brick I didn't throw through your windshield
is stuck in my body,
behind my right shoulder
wedged between the ribs —
a brush stroke of maroon
on an unfinished canvas
painted by a jester
whose hands I can't see.

Every molecule
on the green and blue oasis
of our planet flying through space
is the canvas.
Every molecule is the barrier
between what is
and what could be.

Every atom knows that you love me
in chaparral, under aspen
on soft olive hills
as you let go of my hand.

And now I am on the other side of the moon.
You might not see me again for 2,000 years.
You are in a silent world
of green fire,
sleeping alone.
Not aware of my breathing
between the snow crystals.
Not aware of my heartbeat
like a small animal hiding.
Or maybe it was a snow leopard
walking over the glass roof
of my house
while I was dreaming.
The goats, the shadow,
the Himalayan bells.

I made a decision
to feel everything,
trusting that the universe is not designed
to give me more than I can handle,
to accept everything I do
as a way to learn.

It was a hole in the chalkboard
a path textured through
a newly opened void
with its small net of stars
as crows fly out of the window
the gauze curtain waving
to the moon
like a kata draped over the painted arms
of a goddess.
Or maybe it was a vision
of blood on the mouth of the cave
the buffalo etched with a torch
onto the rippled stone wall
where the fire is burning.

The decision I would have made
to be with you
is stuck in my left shoulder,
but the emotion moves in waves
soft, wet and green
through my whole body,
a cottonwood tree taking root
before its branches twist upward.

Once again,
your hands are tied together
only to themselves.
Your hands are unaware
of what your feet are dreaming.
Your muscles are unaware
of where they haven't danced
before they got distracted.
Once again,
my shoulder is leading me
on a path through apple leaves
away from you.

THE ALL NIGHT
YEMENITE CAFE

The Seduction of Bathsheba

1.
When the King saw her bathing
in the watercolor shades of evening,
dark skin and white steam rising
scented with hyssop and chamomile,
he became obsessed with the way
the hills and valleys of her body
rose and fell
in a sacred dance of falling leaves.

In her, he worshipped
the deep purple of the grape
before it is pressed into wine,
the bright orange of the lily,
the shape of stars,
their force fields,
and the vectors that connect them
to warriors
above the hills of Jerusalem.

Later, when his servants came for her
and her husband disappeared
into a flock of goats,
the edges of the sunset blurred,
purple, dripping and surprised
over a canvas obsessed
with the blue iridescence
of tree frogs.

At midnight
the King was barefoot,
on the balcony,
pushing his way up
through a field of lilies,
brown and ochre streets in the distance,
azaleas in the alley,
goats running madly in all directions.

2.
In the beginning
she was married to the muse,
but it became hard not to touch him,
even though the goats were running
in the opposite direction,
brown and ochre in the distance.

The summer was voluptuous in its dancing.
She gave the muse a tambourine
while she painted desert flowers
and tree frogs in clay alleys.

Sometimes she danced with him,
and sometimes by herself,
after midnight
with delicate silver anklets
on her feet.

At first the music of silver
against silver
was atonal,
but it condensed into
a pointillist painting in the leaves,
transforming the pain
into music.

3.
Her dreams were half in the ice,
half underwater.
A Yemenite bride inside a band of scimitars.
A sculpture of the whirling
energy of emerging leaves.

She told the King
she would always have two lovers,
one emotional and one artistic.
But the lover and the artist began dancing.
First in small silver steps.
Later in a love dance of wild leaping.

The ice became feather thin,
patterned with feathers.
Peacock blue,
the color of longing.
Green and gold,
the color of lucid sleep.
The night was translucent with windows
as they fell through the borders of flowers,
the edges of tambourines,
and Shabazi music
in a wild and feathery leap.

She landed
the way a prima ballerina floats
down to the swans
after a lift.
His strong, muscular arms
guided her
to the molecules of paint
as they condensed
into a landscape that was wildly sensual,
vibrantly creative,
and very silent.

4.
During the eclipse
he lay on his back under eucalyptus trees
watching the shadows condense
into tiny points of light
shaped like crescent moons.

He thought he heard a warning
in the tiny crescents of light,
the bands of shadow,
the dark hole in the sky.

On the hills above Jerusalem,
a prophet was talking to God
inside a cloud
as the rain condensed
into Babylonian cities,
a nation in exile.

49

5.
Centuries later, the King's bride
is still spinning watercolors
out of the edges of her dreams.
She is the ballerina with wild black hair,
the Yemenite smile,
and Russian dancer eyes.

Her people walk across the desert
to a city that has her name.
Colors flow out in earth tones
as she brushes her lips
across the thin membrane of wandering.

Goats graze on the borders
of the invisible.
Lizards skitter up the crevices
of sandstone walls.
Tree frogs disappear
underwater.

She is almost invisible
when she dances
in the Bedouin market.
Silk scarves and harem pants
the color of desert flowers
ripple like a mirage,
but the hills remember
earthtone spices in the open air,
the color of her skin.

Letters from Tel Aviv during the War

1.
My friend calls from Tel Aviv
during the war.
He tells me about the sealed room
in his small apartment,
first the bathroom, then the kitchen —
and the air raids late at night
or two hours before his dreams are finished
in the early morning.
Last winter
he found a small oval stone
in the ruins of a concentration camp in Austria.
He was walking there with school children.
If you look at the rock long enough,
you can see a face.

2.
Half way around the world
it's my birthday. He steps out
from behind the sea turtles
and whispers,
"Lean towards the gardenias."
Before we dance he weaves
red carnations into my hair.
The rosebud on my bed
is for later.
In the silent place
before I dream
he sings about circles.
Then we dive.
Turtle dreams.
Underwater.

3.
The stone arrives in the mail
from Tel Aviv.
I remember naked soldiers
leaping into the waterfall at Ein Gedi,
their uniforms
softly sculptured into leaves
on the rocks.
In the photograph
he is falling out of the sky,
prayer flags attached to his ankles
like a Buddhist monk
in a calmer place.
He says the birds always whisper to him
up there.

4.
An American Jewish friend sends me a silver bead
and asks me to wear it around my neck
on a braided red string.
300 years ago it was a bullet.
He found it in Thailand in a tiny shop
by incense offerings to Buddha
almost hidden between
hammered silver boxes from the hill tribes.
Children collected them
after the French soldiers left,
and for 300 years
they changed a lot of hands.
Now, he says, they are symbols of simplicity
and the cyclicalness of our lives.
Then he said something about endings,
but the kind that lead to new beginnings.
He says if I wear this bullet,
somehow people will remember.

5.
I remember travelling in Thailand,
walking through a small village
on the day of a festival.
A colorful parade
was winding down narrow streets
with the scent of exotic spices,
rows of food vendors,
and dragons jumping from the rooftops.
I remember the stone slab walkway through the temple
and the cinnamon robes of the Buddhist monks.
My friends were teaching me phrases in Thai
and then laughing at my pronunciation.
It was the night before a different war.

6.
My mother calls late at night
after the first Scud missiles hit Tel Aviv.
Also friends from San Francisco
with news of Ze'ev, Aviva, Yael, Eitan.
There was a big chill back in New Jersey.
Also, a large find of sand dollars
on Ocean Beach,
a few hundred feet to the right
of the Taraval Tunnel.
The echo wasn't working properly
that day.

Driving South to the Dead Sea

We were apart for more than five years, except for
a hidden place where I sometimes saw you in dreams.
Now, we're driving south to the Dead Sea, talking in
Hebrew and English, listening to love songs on the radio.

We stop at the Bedouin Market at Ber-Sheva. I
want a teapot, something for my home. A Moroccan
merchant waves to me. His clay pots are shaped by hand,
glazed with three shades of blue, the ancient buildings of
Jerusalem painted in pastels above the Temple Wall. You
bargain with him, from 15 shekels to 10, and buy it for
me. Later you tell me you could have gotten it for 8 if
you had waited longer.

After a lunch of salads, eggplant, carrots, olives,
hummos, mangos, felafel and pita bread at a small outdoor
cafe, we walk around the old part of the city. The flowers
on the trees are so lavender, so brilliantly pink. Two
young men step into my photograph, thinking I want to
photograph them instead of the trees. One of them pees
on the wall and says, "Picture of my ass." Maybe he
thinks I don't understand.

Then we continue south to the Dead Sea, driving
below sea level on land, past caves with desert animals
and hidden Essene scrolls. Carved desert monuments,
sandy and gold. The Dead Sea turquoise as the sky in the
distance.

At night we go out on the roof of the hotel, then
down an unlit stairway to the beach, where our hands are
beginning to remember each other under the moonlight.
The stars above us — the Bear, Casseopeia, and a shooting
star that runs halfway across the sky before it destroys
itself.

My body remembers you completely. I fall into a sleep in the lighted space between us, suspended between two continents. But in the middle of the night, I wake up doubting everything. My memories, my dreams, my intuition, even myself. And the window you closed and locked to protect against terrorists. I had wanted it open.

Hiking with Ya'alim

Hiking to the top
of the waterfall at Ein Gedi,
we decide to go further
up rocks and walls of stone
to King David's Spring.

I am searching for scrolls
hidden in caves by the cliffs
that surround the Dead Sea.
My eyes are almost blinded
by sunlight reflected on the water —
salty, blue and white
in the distance.

I rub my fingers across
the bottom of mineral pools,
the rippled underside of rocks,
look for messages
in the sounds of Hebrew words.

I stare into the eyes
of small deerlike animals
Israelis call ya'alim,
horns like invisible music
curving before their soft brown heads.

We walk barefoot into a small cave
almost hidden by Shulamite vines
hanging down from the rocks
dripping with water.
We feel our way in the semi-dark,
searching for fossils
shards of pottery
Kabbalistic symbols.

Later, we float
belly down
in the Dead Sea,
your feet bent towards the sky,

your arms and legs spread
like you are diving from an airplane,
your wide paratrooper muscles
suspended easily.

In the evening
you make me dinner —
tomatoes, cucumbers
a soft cheese called T'nuva
hummos and bread.
Later, watermelon, cakes and tea
with your brothers.

Dalit tells me about the Scud missile attacks —
five minutes warning,
then the whistle, the rush of air, the crash
and the explosions,
watching through masks
as the tiles fall off the ceiling,
the baby crawling around
in a plastic cage.

Sometimes I feel
your eyes are wounded
by what you have seen —
eleven dead soldiers
wrapped together with a chain,
their names
carved on a rock,
free falling
from 14,000 feet in the air.
Stones large enough to kill
thrown at tourists in Jerusalem.

I know your eyes still want to see
the things that artists see,
and they will reward you
for feeding them with beauty.

So here we are
sitting on the roof
naked
at 2:00 in the morning.

We talk
and watch the birds
fly up against the moonlight —
dark and sandy shadows.

Suddenly, I can't remember
any of my dreams.

The All Night Yemenite Cafe

We've been walking around Jaffa late at night,
on pilgrimage to everything
that artists want to see —
the ancient well by the art center,
walled walks below clusters of lights
like Babylonian flowers or ancient moons,
fishing boats by the harbor,
the Mediterranean Sea,
and the night sky of Tel Aviv
from an elevated walkway.
Artist galleries, murals, fish restaurants,
and hidden places for kisses.

In that deep melodic voice
that reminds me of everything I like in a man,
he tells me the wild crowd gathers
at Nargila, the All Night Yemenite Cafe,
after 2:00 in the morning.
He tells the waitress we want to sit outside,
and she hands him a 12-page menu.
He opens it from the back
and shows me a picture
of a dark man and a blonde woman
feasting on each other.
He says it helps the appetite,
makes you hungry.

He turns the pages slowly
to show me erotic pictures and wild poems
between the prices of the food.
Naked women next to ancient Yemenite treats.
While our food is being cooked,
he translates an article from the Late Evening News
telling how the religious tried to close the place down,
but the City Council said there wasn't a law against it.
Below this, the owner's response
is framed by naked women.
He says the restaurant has two menus
and "yekes" can order from the other one.
That's an Israeli word that sort of means "nerd."

59

Besides, the Yemenite restaurant next door
with the regular menu is always empty.

We order eggplant, pitas,
and a Yemenite treat called "Ziva."
It's curved like a snake,
but has a woman's name.

Two 17-year-old boys come into the outdoor cafe.
They're laughing, looking at the menu,
reading every word,
and trying to think of something to order
so they can keep looking at the pictures.
It's 3:00 in the morning by now.
A group of tourists come in
and ask if they have a different menu.
The waitress says, "I can give you
the one for people under fourteen."

Since it's my first time,
the waitress gives me a bumper sticker
that says "Nargila, where they sell pleasure
and Yemenite food."
I think about putting it on my car in Iowa —
something completely wild
that the fundamentalists can't read
and wouldn't understand if they could.
But my friend says Hebrew letters
might make me a target for terrorists
even there.

The food is so spicy it makes me burn
and stirs my appetite for deeper things.
He is Yemenite too, so I bite his fingers.
Now we're hungry for dessert,
so we drive home through the almost deserted
streets of Tel Aviv
for something much better than food.
And in the morning
after three hours of sleep,
we both wake up laughing.

Images of the North

I. The Road to Hararit

I think reading my palm
was his way
of whispering to angels.

I was raking hay,
and it was making my nose
run constantly.
The gardens were full of bougainvillea,
sculpture, and patterned shade.
Haim was painting huge canvasses
of lavender and poppies.
Shimon had learned another language.

We drove to Hararit
at the end of a sunset
you called "sof olam" —
floating colors at the end of the world.

At the end of a winding road,
a small village
surrounded by olive trees
and Arab families in the valley.
An oasis from the attitudes
in this part of the world.

Dorit tells me
that after the first day of the war,
people sat on top of their houses each night
and watched the missiles fall in white arcs
towards Haifa and Tel Aviv
instead of going to shelters.
They knew if something terrible happened
the masks wouldn't help.

At night you sing to me on the balcony
with your warm Yemenite voice —
Hebrew songs,
the ones we used to dance to.

61

My body remembers —
waves, stone islands,
the contours of your body,
easily familiar.

In my sleep I am riding
on the road from Metulla to Sfat
with friends, windows wide open
and "Higher Love" playing loud
on the car stereo,
serious barbed wire
swirling
three feet thick
at the Lebanese border.

An immigrant artist invites me
into the edges of her watercolors.
Later, in her gallery
a Kaballistic rabbi reads my palm.
He predicts a bright future for me,
later, somewhere else.

II. White Deer

I remember the night I was lost in the forest
in my own country. The moon rose high
above the mist where I waited
in an open field.
And I shivered while the hours passed slowly
until morning.

White deer came to lick my fingers
in the slanted morning light,
but as I hiked back to the trail,
I knew that something deeper
than the late night chill
had frozen.

But now
in the middle of the night
I meet you by a field of plum-colored grapes
surrounded by high stone walls.
There is a message —
Hebrew letters carved into rocks
with sky on the other side.

The letters
are like lines in a palm,
curved, and full of music.
Later I am wading in the Kinneret,
looking for jasper stones
in shallow water.

III. In the Negev

Several years ago,
the Israelis invented a car
called the Susita —
the Middle Eastern answer to Detroit.
Because of the price of metals,
they made the body out of fiberglass
and painted it in the colors of summer flowers.

But if anyone left a Susita
in the desert
to go hiking in the Negev,
the camels would eat it!
My Kibbutz friends explained
that camels have very strong digestion.
They ate the fiberglass,
even the seats.
Then when the hikers returned,
all they would find were lumps of metal
sitting there —
the spontaneous sculpture of a melting sun.

IV. Air Lift

Melodic voices from radios
swirl up from the alleys.
15,000 Falasha refugees have just
been airlifted from Ethiopia.
Most of them didn't know they were coming here
until yesterday. We turn on the TV
and watch them being helped onto planes
by soldiers without uniforms.

They came with nothing
but the clothes they were wearing
and their children.
Seven mothers gave birth on the airplanes,
and most had never seen a plane before.

I watch their eyes
as the visions they had prayed for
suddenly become real.
Tomorrow they'll go to Jerusalem
to pray at the Western Wall —
the abode of compassion
in a war zone.

V. White Lilies

Back in Tel Aviv
a young Israeli soldier
walks down Dizengoff with a machine gun
hanging on one shoulder,
a girl hanging on the other,
and a guitar
dangling across his chest,
the two of them kissing,
oblivious to the machine gun.

Below the slatted windows
in your apartment,
seven vermillion roses
and a stem of white lilies
by our bed,
their sweet scent mixing
with the music of our bodies.

But this will all dissolve.

Months later
a handful of pebbles
I collect at Muir Beach
will fall out of an envelope
halfway around the world,
jade and jasper
in your hand.

Better by Moonlight

"There are some flowers that bloom
better by moonlight than in the sun."
— Bernard Soulie
Japanese Eroticism

It's one of those perfect moments —
after dark, but early enough
to have my eyes wide open,
part of the moon in the sky
with a halo around it,
predicting tomorrow's heat.

We leave our car by the beach,
next to a stone tower.
In the garden you show me
small yellow flowers called "Ner Ha'Laila" —
candles of the night.
The blossoms open at night
and only once.
By the morning, they're gone.

You ask me to say it with you,
"Ner Ha'Laila."

We walk by the sand dunes
arm in arm
to a place where
hundreds of people are dancing
on the beach —
samba and lambada
some in uniform
some younger
all of them wild.

The lights of Jaffa
are amber in the distance
as we walk back.

Later I paint my lips
with raspberries,
put the juice in your mouth.

When you pull me
close to you
the music still lifts us
like the white birds we saw
flying in slow circles
above the Mediterranean Sea.

Bright yellow flowers
are blooming between the stones,
their supernova petals
stronger than the stars
I can cover with my fingers.

You call me "Ner Ha'Laila,"
your Middle Eastern dancer,
your Japanese temple fire
late at night.

You open my petals,
drop ripples
into the place where
the sky is born.

I am the flower that blooms
only for you
only at night
and
only once.

By morning, it's gone.

Looking at Photographs

Machine guns change people.
Bombs explode them from the inside
like clusters of bougainvillea
blowing apart. Fragments of petals
above an ancient house in ruins
by the Mediterranean Sea.
But we have been exploring the stones.

After I came back to my own country,
I looked at photographs.
Five years ago
when you were here with me,
I saw a sensitivity
and vulnerability in your face
that has flown away like doves
escaping from a waterfall
before the water is dammed
upriver,
pushed out by long hours working.
Studying at night.
Little time for sleep.

Even then, you had
the strongest and sweetest muscles
I had ever seen on a man,
the tannest skin,
and a passion
that can only come
to those who dare to penetrate
the soft hollow space
beneath the spines of cactus.

Your body took a different shape
in its ancient home.
Personal boundaries more defined,
lines etched deeper.
Extra weight in strength
and armor.
My friend says it's for protection,
and you need it there.

69

You, the one whose name means "strong."
You, the one who taught me
how to protect myself in my own country.
You, the one who said,
"Put your pack in front of your face
if they throw stones,"
when we were in Jerusalem
a few hours after
three women were killed by terrorists.

Still, you loved my softness
and my vulnerability.
You went diving for the metallic fish
in my soft mountain pools.
It mystified you how strange words
kept flying into me
unannounced,
and you tried to transform each day
into a poem. You planned
each detail carefully, artistically.
And you loved the way
I got so excited
about everything I heard and saw —
the Mediterranean seaside below a quarter moon,
the lights of Jaffa
glowing gold in the distance,
narrow streets named after animals in the sky.

Each day, we gave each other gifts,
mint leaves, laughter,
words in three different languages.
But our paths diverged three years ago.
Strong cords bind you to an ancient place
that would destroy me over time.
And when I wanted words from you,
you could only show me.

You always take me to the airport
with your unborn children
in the soft and hollow places
where I am most vulnerable.
You're always the one
who has to be strong for both of us.

This time we've completed a cycle,
and I don't know if we'll meet again
in this life, or this body.

An older friend tries to comfort me.
He says, "Your artistic roots are in America.
Poets need peace.
You would be short-circuited by all that violence."
He says, "Your dreams will heal you,
over time."

Something is empty now
where too much was written before,
an unexplored depth
that used to be tangled with weeds.
But I'm planting flowers there
Shasta daisies, calla lilies
honeysuckle vines.

Secret Places

I wanted to give you a few weeks
of something more
than you had known before —
a sultry Mediterranean heat,
rocks from the Dead Sea,
cascading molecules
from the waterfall at Ein Gedi.

I wanted to airbrush you
inside one of the mystical paintings
of Sfat,
to find you inside the lines
of a Kaballistic rabbi's palm.
I wanted to rub your feet
with oil pressed out of a coconut,
to show you the secret places
inside the pyramids.

I knew that even a small amount of this
would make you
different.

She knew it too.
When I went halfway around the world,
she made her bed soft
with feathers and rose petals.

I almost knew
as I gathered mint leaves
and watched
the rain from my open window.

I wanted to love you like a thunderstorm
in August.
Cicadas leaping away from the path
to the bridge over the pond,
tree frogs underwater.

Always at the appropriate moment
I break an alarm clock,

lose a watch,
or forget where I am going.

I've been losing jackets,
shedding leaves,
losing all my layers
of protection.

A friend tells me to culture patience.
Distance is only an illusion.
Lean towards the abundance,
he says. Magnolias
opening in the summer.

The body remembers
as if there were no distance
or time. A leaf,
or a stem
tracing the landscape
of your body.

I forget where I am going.
Leaves, stems, gardenias.
A humid summer evening
where everything
dissolves.

And opens
into a landscape of gardenias
where the ideas that were abandoned
in a darker place
are always taking form,
shape and color.

You'll find the thousand kisses
I never gave you
hidden in moon slivers
just before the early morning light.

Seven Clowns Swimming across the Sky

1.
You shine your headlights
in my window
to see me dancing.

I hold your letter close to my heart,
shake out leaves from narrow sidewalks
in Jaffa
onto my sheets,
paint cactus spines
in watercolor.

The music I hear comes from Egypt
or a small cafe
on the north side of Tel Aviv.
It makes me think of you walking
thousands of years ago
in the Fertile Crescent
with your arms full of
hyacinths
orange melons
lemons spilling out of a basket.
Maybe I knew you there.

2.
A clown dances at my window
in a smiling red bow tie
that glows in the dark.
Certain things that he does
and doesn't do
hurt me.

We kiss in the shadows of music
from the car radio,
in a yard full of bougainvillea,
the back stairs
half illumined by the streetlight.
The wooden steps lead to
something I can't hear yet.

He always gives me sweet things
when he leaves —
jelly donuts
blueberry cheesecake
pirouette chocolate biscuits —
things to choke on.

3.
The astronomer
has just offered to name
a plasma planet
after me —
if one can be discovered
and somewhere in the universe
exists.

For a few moments
the vectors
collide in space
melting
then bouncing off
a blue clown
in opposite directions.

The force field pulls at my heart
and leaves a hole in my chest.

4.
The Viking Warrior
pierces the edges of my dream.
He reaches into the middle
of a love night
swimming
through the asteroids.
He writes
"Goddess of the Blue Light"
in the mist on my windshield.

When he puts his hands on my head
to bless me
the light penetrates.

5.
During the terrorist attack
an old Arab man
led my friend out of Jerusalem
through back alleys.
The 14-year-old
with the Molotov cocktails
looked confused.
He tried to glaze the hesitation
out of his eyes
moments before throwing.

The old man said,
"Follow me.
Walk slowly.
Don't look back."

6.
The red satin bow in my hair
is electric tonight.
My dancing shoes are silver.
I pirouette in the shadows
with an invisible partner.

The astronaut says, "You are loved
more than even you can imagine."
His voice bounces
off my rear view mirror,
shatters
the face of my watch
where the hands of small animals
are telling me
time to dance.